EROSION

PRINCETON SERIES OF CONTEMPORARY POETS

For Other Books in the Series, see page 84

EROSION

BY JORIE GRAHAM

PRINCETON UNIVERSITY PRESS • PRINCETON, NEW JERSEY

Copyright © 1983 by Princeton University Press

Published by Princeton University Press, Princeton, New Jersey
In the United Kingdom: Princeton University Press, Chichester, West Sussex

Library of Congress Cataloging in Publication Data

Graham, Jorie, 1951-
Erosion.

(Princeton series of contemporary poets)
I. Title. II. Series.
PS3557.R214E7 1983   811'.54   82-61365
ISBN 0-691-06570-5 ISBN 0-691-01405-1 (pbk.)

Publication of this book has been aided by a grant from The Whitney
Darrow Publication Reserve Fund of Princeton University Press

This book has been composed in Linotron Sabon

Princeton University Press books are printed on acid-free paper
and meet the guidelines for permanence and durability of the Committee on
Production Guidelines for Book Longevity of the Council on Library Resources

Printed in the United States of America by Princeton Academic Press

Designed by Laury A. Egan

10   9   8

CONTENTS

FOR JIM

ACKNOWLEDGMENTS

Grateful acknowledgment is made to the editors of the following journals in which these poems first appeared:

ANTAEUS

San Sepolcro
The Daffodil
Massacio's Expulsion
Scirocco

THE AMERICAN POETRY REVIEW

Wanting a Child
Erosion
The Age of Reason
Reading Plato
In What Manner the Body is
    United with the Soule
Wood Wasps in the Spanish
    Willow
At Luca Signorelli's Resurrection
    of the Body
Patience
At the Long Island Jewish
    Geriatric Home
Two Paintings by Gustav Klimt
The Sense of an Ending

THE IOWA REVIEW

I Watched a Snake
Mist
To a Friend Going Blind

THE NATION

The Lady and the Unicorn and
    Other Tapestries

PLOUGHSHARES

Kimono

NEW ENGLAND REVIEW

My Garden, My Daylight
    (reprinted in the Pushcart
    Anthology, 1982)
On Form for Berryman (Jan 7,
    1982)
At the Exhumed Body of
    Santa Chiara, Assisi

MISSOURI REVIEW

For John Keats
Salmon

IRONWOOD

Making a Living
Love
History
Mother of Vinegar

THE REAPER

Tragedy

PEQUOD

Still Life with Window and Fish
Of Unevenness

I would also like to thank the Ingram-Merrill Foundation and the Bunting Institute at Radcliffe College for Fellowships that aided me in the completion of this book.

EROSION

SAN SEPOLCRO

In this blue light
    I can take you there,
snow having made me
    a world of bone
seen through to. This
    is my house,

my section of Etruscan
    wall, my neighbor's
lemontrees, and, just below
    the lower church,
the airplane factory.
    A rooster

crows all day from mist
    outside the walls.
There's milk on the air,
    ice on the oily
lemonskins. How clean
    the mind is,

holy grave. It is this girl
    by Piero
della Francesca, unbuttoning
    her blue dress,
her mantle of weather,
    to go into

labor. Come, we can go in.
    It is before
the birth of god. No-one
    has risen yet
to the museums, to the assembly
    line—bodies

and wings—to the open air
　　market. This is
what the living do: go in.
　　It's a long way.
And the dress keeps opening
　　from eternity

to privacy, quickening.
　　Inside, at the heart,
is tragedy, the present moment
　　forever stillborn,
but going in, each breath
　　is a button

coming undone, something terribly
　　nimble-fingered
finding all of the stops.

MIST

This quick intelligence that only knows
distracted, blind,
poking like a nose,
forever trying to finger the distinctions: *the rose*
that opens in the rose,
that opens in
the mist,
its geography

much quicker than
its history.
I live in it, it lives in me, whore to, heir to,
I am the one it does unto. . . .
And this is its shoreline: the edge of the continent, of the whole
idea, the ragged rocks
becoming foam,

where the sky drops this low each day to fish for us.
It should burn off, they say,
yet see it eat
the bony rocks,
its fog-flesh making everything
part of itself until

I am the fish that ate the fish that ate the littlest,
in thought,
in afterthought;
swimming the one world deaf, waving, goodbye for motor,
fish that can't hear
itself swim, its hum
in the water;

swimming this other as
the rose inside the rose that keeps on opening; and then
this other still
wherein it is a perfect rose
because I snap it
from the sky,

because I want it,

another, thicker, kind of sight.

READING PLATO

This is the story
        of a beautiful
lie, what slips
        through my fingers,
your fingers. It's winter,
        it's far

in the lifespan
        of man.
Bareheaded, in a soiled
        shirt,
speechless, my friend
        is making

lures, his hobby. Flies
        so small
he works with tweezers and
        a magnifying glass.
They must be
        so believable

they're true—feelers,
        antennae,
quick and frantic
        as something
drowning. His heart
        beats wildly

in his hands. It is
        blinding
and who will forgive him
        in his tiny
garden? He makes them
        out of hair,

deer hair, because it's hollow
        and floats.
Past death, past sight,
        this is

his good idea, what drives
    the silly days

together. Better than memory. Better
    than love.
Then they are done, a hook
    under each pair
of wings, and it's Spring,
    and the men

wade out into the riverbed
    at dawn. Above,
the stars still connect-up
    their hungry animals.
Soon they'll be satisfied
    and go. Meanwhile

upriver, downriver, imagine, quick
    in the air,
in flesh, in a blue
    swarm of
flies, our knowledge of
    the graceful

deer skips easily across
    the surface.
Dismembered, remembered,
    it's finally
alive. Imagine
    the body

they were all once
    a part of,
these men along the lush
    green banks
trying to slip in
    and pass

for the natural world.

SCIROCCO

In Rome, at 26
        Piazza di Spagna,
at the foot of a long
        flight of
stairs, are rooms
        let to Keats

in 1820,
        where he died. Now
you can visit them,
        the tiny terrace,
the bedroom. The scraps
        of paper

on which he wrote
        lines
are kept behind glass,
        some yellowing,
some xeroxed or
        mimeographed. . . .

Outside his window
        you can hear the scirocco
working
        the invisible.
Every dry leaf of ivy
        is fingered,

refingered. Who is
        the nervous spirit
of this world
        that must go over and over
what it already knows,
        what is it

so hot and dry
        that's looking through us,
by us,
        for its answer?
In the arbor
        on the terrace

the stark hellenic
        forms
of grapes have appeared.
        They'll soften
till weak enough
        to enter

our world, translating
        helplessly
from the beautiful
        to the true. . . .
Whatever the spirit,
        the thickening grapes

are part of its looking,
        and the slow hands
that made this mask
        of Keats
in his other life,
        and the old woman,

the memorial's
        custodian,
sitting on the porch
        beneath the arbor
sorting chick-peas
        from pebbles

into her cast-iron
        pot.
See what her hands
        know—
they are its breath,
        its mother

tongue, dividing,
        discarding.
There is light playing
        over the leaves,
over her face,
        making her

abstract, making
        her quick
and strange. But she
        has no care
for what speckles her,
        changing her,

she is at
        her work. Oh how we want
to be taken
        and changed,
want to be mended
        by what we enter.

Is it thus
        with the world?
Does it wish us
        to mend it,
light and dark,
        green

and flesh? Will it
    be free then?
I think the world
    is a desperate
element. It would have us
    calm it,

receive it. Therefore this
    is what I
must ask you
    to imagine: wind;
the moment
    when the wind

drops; and grapes,
    which are nothing,
which break
    in your hands.

IN WHAT MANNER THE BODY
IS UNITED WITH THE SOULE

Finally I heard
     into music,
that is, heard past
     the surface tension
which is pleasure, which holds
     the self

afloat, miraculous
     waterstrider
with no other home.
     Not that I heard
very deep,
     but heard there was a depth,

a space through which
     you could fall,
an echo travel,
     and meaning
—small, jeweled, deep-water—
     flash. I heard

in a piano concerto
     the distance between the single instrument
and the whole
     republic,
heard the argument each made
     for fate,

free will.
     And listened
to the piano, solo,
     on its gold hook, the tip
of the baton,
     struggle

and struggle.

2.

From the mud
    of the Arno
in winter, 1967,
    we pulled up
manuscripts
    illuminated by monks

in tenth century
    monasteries.
Sometimes the gold letters loosened
    into the mud,
into our hands.
    We found

elaborate gold frames,
    Annunciations,
candlesticks. The ice
    the mud became
along the banks caught
    bits of sun

and gleamed.
    Eddies, twists, baroque knots
of currents,
    all the difficulties
of the passage
    of time

caught and held
    in the lush browns
we reached through
    blindly
for relics. It was
    almost spring,

we waded out further,
    the bells
in the churches

        kept up
their small
        warnings. The self, too,

is an act of
        rescue
where the flesh has risen,
        the spirit
loosened. . . .

                3.

Upstream the river
        is smaller,
almost still.
        On a warm day
the silence of the surface holds
        its jewels,

its tiny insect
        life.
In silence the waterstriders
        measure ripples
for meaning.
        They catch the bee

that has just touched
        the surface
accidentally. In silence
        the strider
and the backswimmer
        (its mirror image

underwater, each
        with ventral surface toward
the waterfilm)
        share the delicate
gold bee. They can both,
        easily,

be satisfied. They feed.
    Sun shines.
Of silence, mating striders make
    gold eggs
which they will only lay
    on feathers

dropped by passing birds
    or on the underside
of a bird's tail
    before it wakens and
flies off, blue and white and host
    to a freedom

it knows nothing of.

THE AGE OF REASON

1.

The anxious bird in the wild
    spring green
is *anting*, which means,
    in my orchard
he has opened his wings
    over a furious

anthill and will take up
    into the delicate
ridges of quince-yellow
    feathers
a number of tiny, angry
    creatures

that will inhabit him, bewildered
    no doubt,
traveling deep
    into the air
on this feathery planet,
    new life. . . .

We don't know why
    they do it.
At times they'll take on
    almost anything
that burns, spreading
    their wings

over coals, over cigarette
    butts,
even, mistakenly, on bits
    of broken glass.
Meanwhile the light keeps
    stroking them

as if it were love. The garden
    continues its work

all round them, the gradual
    openings that stand
for death. Under the plastic
    groundcover the human

garden grows: help-sticks
    and knots, row
after row. Who wouldn't want
    to take
into the self
    something that burns

or cuts, or wanders
    lost
over the body?

2.

At the end of Werner Herzog's
    Woyzek,
after the hero whom
    we love
who is mad has
    murdered

the world, the young
    woman
who is his wife,
    and loved her,
and covered himself
    with blood,

he grows frightened
    by how quickly
she softens and takes on the shape
    of the soil.
In the moonlight he throws
    his knife

into the wide river
    flowing beside them
but doesn't think it has
    reached deep
enough so goes in
    after it

himself. White as a knife,
    he goes in after it
completely. The trees are green.
    The earth
is green. The light
    is sick

with green. Now that
    he's gone
the woman is a tiny
    gap
in green. Next day,
    in slow

motion, the undertakers and
    philosophers
(it is the Age of
    Reason)
wander through the tall
    and glossy

ferns and grasses
    looking for
the instrument. It's spring.
    The air is
gold. Every now and then
    they lift

the white sheet they have
    laid to see
what death is. They are
    meticulous,

the day is everything
    they have.

       3.

How far is true
    enough?
How far into the
    earth
can vision go and
    still be

love? Isn't the
    honesty
of things where they
    resist,
where only the wind
    can bend them

back, the real weather,
    not our
desire hissing Tell me
    your parts
that I may understand
    your body,

your story. Which is why
    we have
characters and the knife
    of a plot
to wade through this
    current. Now

it's blossoms
    back to back
through the orchard.
    A surf
of tenderness. There is
    no deep

enough. For what we want
    to take
inside of us, whole orchard,
    color,
name, scent, symbol, raw
    pale

blossoms, wet black
    arms there is
no deep enough.

AT THE EXHUMED BODY OF
SANTA CHIARA, ASSISI

So here you are, queen of the chiaroscuro, black girl,
backstitching on us. What would you mend coming back up
intact? Is it so crooked a thing
you want us

to see? Here we are, the temporary ones
at your deathsill. The sky over our irreversible progress
impure and sometimes glad
is blue. The sky over whether I leave him

or not, over myth, extermination camps, and Bruna's hands
making lace faster than I
can see, is blue. Blue over your body in its afterlife
on its back in its black dress with gold trim

looking out on us the unused.
As if the flesh were the eternal portion after all,
here it is, your blunt modesty, pure,
even after a ton of dirt, six hundred years,

and the emblem in the human mind
you have become. As if this were always
what flesh is a declension of: more flesh. Beneath motion
more flesh,

beneath daylight and rot and law. . . . Can it be true?
the night wind softening and softening the olive trees till
what I see of them is where they were
just then,

calling that *olive trees*. I touch
that love. That deep delay. So and so you loved,
so and so you left before the age of twenty-one calling it
faith, founding an order of

such nuns, all dressed in black, black veil over
the face. In order not to hide from us, that veil. In order
to be seen.
              I lean upon your nowhere now.

ON FORM FOR BERRYMAN
(Jan 7, 1982)

1.

And what, to you, would it mean, this anniversary?
Backward and forward you flailed, but only horribly
forward you dragged. Were *pulled*
you hoped. Even if only by shape,
by law. So this, ten years, is your full rhyme
old man. It's you now, blurred and breathless.
Anniversary, as in

you can't get away
from the shape of the mess. Its beautiful bone.
The handshake you make with the invisible right at
the start. It keeps its word. And drives you under
trying to figure what word it was you gave,
what, then, do you owe?
That has to be the plan,

if nothing else: figure the debt, your own exceptional debt,
tossing and thrashing,
hoarding, forgiving and up all night waiting for something
to give. Waiting for the unstrangeness to find you
phrase by phrase, to climb
down through your knots lies chords, your miserable honeyed
beseeching, your skinny arms out
asking for proof,

2.

meaning you've got to be some kind of payment
due. In full. The guy down the hall from me
learning to play his trumpet doing scales
he's got his job: pay back with accuracy, pay
with the one sharp note you learn and then
with the clean one
you don't, the leap

into the crooked song. And the guy in the park
this morning early pushing his daughter in the swing,
he wants to be free,
he wants to owe something,
he pushes her in as if she were a better question
to ask of this light,
he pushes the words

flesh of my flesh which are impossible
up into the playlit playground. He wants to know
love which is mostly giving up
is for what? The swingset trembles from their work.
This is from him who knows you have to hate one thing
and hate it deep and well.
He pushes her up

into the sun which seems irrelevant, her hair
her beautiful fine useless hair, fruit of dumb growth,
up in the air now, for what, he wonders,
for what, this blaze of light that seems to mock him,
this brute afterlife, hair, this remnant
of history the sun
can know itself in.

AT THE LONG ISLAND
JEWISH GERIATRIC HOME

This is the sugar
    you're stealing
from the nurses, filling
    your pillow
with something
    for nothing,
filling my pockets
    till I'm some kind
of sandman
    you can still

send away. As for
    dreams,
your head rustling in
    white ash,
who needs them?
    It's this world
you love,
    the only one
where theft is possible.
    Today

there's mist outside your
    stormwindow.
The trees grow vague,
    then are
completely gone,
    then stain
this world again as it
    evolves
through them.
    Now,

from any window
    I learn
about freedom, from the muscular
    leanings

of any tree, the fate
        of sunlight,
of the wall in the way.
        Out there,
deep in the sleight
        of hand

is where you whipped
        my mother
for a stolen pencilbox
        till they thought
she was dead. And there
        is her sister,
the one who's never cut
        her hair,
and there the one who died leaving
        a freezer full

of meals twenty years old
        or more. Maybe
it's true, maybe there just
        isn't enough
to go around. Though once, when I
        was very small,
you took me out back
        to your tiny
orchard and let me pick
        till I was

bored. You showed me how
        only a tree
can steal (through sap
        and leaves)
the minerals of parent rock
        and feed them
(by the leafrot) to
        the soil.
How that delay (you drew
        a fountain

in the dirt) is all
    we ever
are. *Who wants a handout*
    anyhow,
you say. Family hours
    are almost
up. There is one branch
    I've kept
from there: it's shaped exactly
    like a woman

running, one raised thigh
    smoothed
by wind, and hair (really
    the shoreline
where the limb is almost torn
    away) unraveling.
She looks like she could
    outrun
anything, although of course
    she's stuck

for good here in this
    memory,
and in the myth it calls
    to mind,
and in this late interpretation
    stolen from
a half-remembered tree
    which stands
there still like some god's
    narrow throat

or mind nothing can slit her
    free of.

(IES *1895-1982*)

TO A FRIEND GOING BLIND

Today, because I couldn't find the shortcut through,
I had to walk this town's entire inner
perimeter to find
where the medieval walls break open
in an eighteenth century
arch. The yellow valley flickered on and off
through cracks and the gaps
for guns. Bruna is teaching me
to cut a pattern.
Saturdays we buy the cloth.
She takes it in her hands
like a good idea, feeling
for texture, grain, the built-in
limits. It's only as an afterthought she asks
and do you think it's beautiful?
Her measuring tapes hang down, corn-blond and endless,
from her neck.
When I look at her
I think *Rapunzel,*
how one could climb that measuring,
that love. But I was saying,
I wandered all along the street that hugs the walls,
a needle floating
on its cloth. Once
I shut my eyes and felt my way
along the stone. Outside
is the cashcrop, sunflowers, as far as one can see. Listen,
the wind rattles in them,
a loose worship
seeking an object,
an interruption. Sara,
the walls are beautiful. They block the view.
And it feels rich to be
inside their grasp.
When Bruna finishes her dress
it is the shape of what has come
to rescue her. She puts it on.

TRAGEDY

The boys in my neighbor's yard
are a middle kingdom, They're playing *Keep-*
away. The one who has the ball
is learning luck. I watch them through a scrim:
my windowframe; a row of holly slow
with fruit crossing its branches here and there
with an alchemical young
oak. From here
it seems the game takes place between
these limbs—each young man entering a tree, emerging
emptyhanded. Across the lawn,
at eye level,
my neighbor's sitting in her window seat.
She's turned slightly away, bent over
needlework. Above her house the town is vaguely tiered,
an honest form. And mist
is lowering, wisps catching everywhere
like flags, surrendering.
Sometimes the game will travel
past the frame. I hear them squeal. Then she and I,
each at our gap,
sustain the visible. We are the loom
of empty green
and cries. Of course, it's almost silent
where we are, behind the glass, but of the abstract
of their play we're making
flesh. She's slow
in her repair. The grass can only
grow. You win when everything is used and nothing's
changed is how it was explained
to me.

WANTING A CHILD

How hard it is for the river here to re-enter
the sea, though it's most beautiful, of course, in the waste
of time where it's almost
turned back. Then
it's yoked,
trussed. . . .The river
has been everywhere, imagine, dividing, discerning,
cutting deep into the parent rock,
scouring and scouring
its own bed.
Nothing is whole
where it has been. Nothing
remains unsaid.
Sometimes I'll come this far from home
merely to dip my fingers in this glittering, archaic
sea that renders everything
identical, flesh
where mind and body
blur. The seagulls squeak, ill-fitting
hinges, the beach is thick
with shells. The tide
is always pulsing upward, inland, into the river's rapid
argument, pushing
with its insistent tragic waves—the living echo,
says my book, of some great storm far out at sea, too far
to be recalled by us
but transferred
whole onto this shore by waves, so that erosion
is its very face.

MY GARDEN, MY DAYLIGHT

My neighbor brings me bottom fish—
    tomcod, rockcod—
a fist of ocean. He comes out
    from the appletrees between us
holding his gift like a tight
    spool of thread.

Once a week he brings me fresh-catch,
    boned and skinned
and rolled up like a tongue. I freeze them,
    speechless, angelic
instruments. I have a choir of them.
    Alive, they feed

driving their bodies through the mud,
    mud through their flesh.
See how white they become. High above,
    the water thins
to blue, then air, then less. . . .
    These aren't as sweet

as those that shine up there,
    quick schools
forever trying to slur over, become water.
    But these belong to us
who cannot fall out of this world
    but only deeper

into it, driving it into the white
    of our eyes. Muddy
daylight, we utter it, we drown in it.
    You can stay dry
if you can step between the raindrops
    mother's mother

said. She's words now you can't hear.
    I try to wind my way
between what's here: chalk, lily, milk,
    titanium, snow—

as far as I can say
    these appleblossoms house

five shades of white, and yet
    I know there's more.
Between my held breath and its small hot
    death, a garden,
Whiteness, grows. Its icy fruit
    seems true,

it glows. *For free* he says
    so that I can't refuse.

STILL LIFE WITH WINDOW AND FISH

Down here this morning in my white kitchen
along the slim body
of the light,
the narrow body that would otherwise
say forever
the same thing,
the beautiful interruptions, the things of this world, twigs
and powerlines, eaves and ranking
branches burn
all over my walls.
Even the windowpanes are rich.
The whole world outside
wants to come into here,
to angle into
the simpler shapes of rooms, to be broken and rebroken
against the sure co-ordinates
of walls.
The whole world outside. . . .
I know it's better, whole, outside, the world—whole
trees, whole groves—but I
love it in here where it blurs, and nothing starts or
ends, but all is
waving, and colorless,
and voiceless. . . .
Here is a fish-spine on the sea of my bone china
plate. Here is a fish-spine on the sea of my hand,
flickering, all its freight
fallen away,
here is the reason for motion washed
in kitchenlight, fanning, gliding
upstream in the smoke of twigs, the rake
against the shed outside, the swaying birdcage
and its missing
tenant. If I should die
before you do,

you can find me anywhere
in this floral, featureless,
indelible
surf. We are too restless
to inherit
this earth.

I WATCHED A SNAKE

hard at work in the dry grass
　　behind the house
catching flies. It kept on
　　disappearing.
And though I know this has
　　something to do

with lust, today it seemed
　　to have to do
with work. It took it almost half
　　an hour to thread
roughly ten feet of lawn,
　　so slow

between the blades you couldn't see
　　it move. I'd watch
its path of body in the grass go
　　suddenly invisible
only to reappear a little
　　further on

black knothead up, eyes on
　　a butterfly.
This must be perfect progress where
　　movement appears
to be a vanishing, a mending
　　of the visible

by the invisible—just as we
　　stitch the earth,
it seems to me, each time
　　we die, going
back under, coming back up. . . .
　　It is the simplest

stitch, this going where we must,
　　leaving a not
unpretty pattern by default. But going
　　out of hunger

for small things—flies, words—going
      because one's body

goes. And in this disconcerting creature
      a tiny hunger,
one that won't even press
      the dandelions down,
retrieves the necessary blue-
      black dragonfly

that has just landed on a pod . . .
      all this to say
I'm not afraid of them
      today, or anymore
I think. We are not, were not, ever
      wrong. Desire

is the honest work of the body,
      its engine, its wind.
It too must have its sails—wings
      in this tiny mouth, valves
in the human heart, meanings like sailboats
      setting out

over the mind. Passion is work
      that retrieves us,
lost stitches. It makes a pattern of us,
      it fastens us
to sturdier stuff
      no doubt.

MOTHER OF VINEGAR

Because contained damage makes for beauty, it shines
like a brain at the bottom of each vat, the sand
in the shell,
a simple animal.
There are great ones that have lasted forever,
the memory of some original going sour in a sweet world
kept intact—
though now this is the taste we love best, its lush
righteousness.
Here we have a ragged bit of one
old as the Declaration
of Independence,
and once a month I hold it to the light
watching for vinegar eels,
their gold script.
To last, my document must remain
mute, a reddish continent breathing its slower time
into the water's eager, thinner
flesh, until finally
it can heal anything, this water with its mother
in its belly, our cheapest
ingredient, the river
of households. It says
we are best clean with what claims everything
indifferently—bruises, nightmares,
coffee stains on linen.
The barnyard animals are healed by it, and windows,
and greens,
and my hair
which shines in the wind over my body
like our flag
on the moon.

THE LADY AND THE UNICORN
AND OTHER TAPESTRIES

If I have a faith it is something like this: this ordering
    of images
within an atmosphere that will receive them, hold them
    in solution, unsolved.
It is this: that the quail
over the snow

on our back field run free and clocklike, briefly safe.
That they rise up in gusts, stiff and atemporal, the moment
    a game they enter,
held in place, as prey,
by goodness,

by their role in the design. And when they rise, straight up,
to this or that limb in the snowfat fir, they seem
    —because the body drops
so far below its wings—
to also fall,

like our best lies that make what's absolutely volatile
look like it's weighted down—our whitest lie, *the beautiful.* . . .
    They rise up in
the falling snow,
and yet to see them is to see

their fallenness. . . . And when, each to their limb they go,
their faces taupe and indigo and peeking gently out
    from under hats like thread
and needle starting to
pull in the simple

fear, it is an ancient tree their eager eyes map out—
playful and vengeful and symmetry-bound: where out of love
    the quail are woven
into tapestries, and, stuffed
with cardamon and pine-nuts

and a sprig of thyme.

KIMONO

The woman on the other side
    of the evergreens
a small boy is hidden in,
    I'm wearing
valleys, clear skies,
    thawing banks

narcissus and hollow reeds
    break through.
It means the world to him, this flat
    archaic fabric
no weather worries.
    Each time I bend,

brushing my hair, a bird
    has just dipped
through its sky out of
    sight. He thinks
I don't see him, my little man
    no more than seven

catching his lost stitch of breath.
    What he sees,
in my garden, is the style
    of the world
as she brushes her hair
    eternally beyond

the casual crumbling forms
    of boughs. I bend
and reeds are suddenly
    ravines. . . . How soothing
it is, this enchanted gap, this tiny
    eternal

delay which is our knowing,
    our flesh.
How late it is, I think,
    bending,

in this world we have mis—
    taken, late

for the green scrim to be
    such an open
door. And yet, even now, a small
    spirit accurate
as new ice is climbing
    into the gentle limbs

of an evergreen, the scent rubbing off
    on his elbows
and knees, his eyes a sacred store
    of dares,
to watch, as on the other side,
    just past

the abstract branches, something
    most whole
loosens her stays
    pretending she's alone.

SALMON

I watched them once, at dusk, on television, run,
in our motel room half-way through
Nebraska, quick, glittering, past beauty, past
the importance of beauty,
archaic,
not even hungry, not even endangered, driving deeper and deeper
into less. They leapt up falls, ladders,
and rock, tearing and leaping, a gold river
and a blue river traveling
in opposite directions.
They would not stop, resolution of will
and helplessness, as the eye
is helpless
when the image forms itself, upside-down, backward,
driving up into
the mind, and the world
unfastens itself
from the deep ocean of the given. . . . Justice, aspen
leaves, mother attempting
suicide, the white night-flying moth
the ants dismantled bit by bit and carried in
right through the crack
in my wall. . . . How helpless
the still pool is,
upstream,
awaiting the gold blade
of their hurry. Once, indoors, a child,
I watched, at noon, through slatted wooden blinds,
a man and woman, naked, eyes closed,
climb onto each other,
on the terrace floor,
and ride—two gold currents
wrapping round and round each other, fastening,
unfastening. I hardly knew
what I saw. Whatever shadow there was in that world
it was the one each cast
onto the other,
the thin black seam

they seemed to be trying to work away
between them. I held my breath.
As far as I could tell, the work they did
with sweat and light
was good. I'd say
they traveled far in opposite
directions. What is the light
at the end of the day, deep, reddish-gold, bathing the walls,
the corridors, light that is no longer light, no longer clarifies,
illuminates, antique, freed from the body of
the air that carries it. What is it
for the space of time
where it is useless, merely
beautiful? When they were done, they made a distance
one from the other
and slept, outstretched,
on the warm tile
of the terrace floor,
smiling, faces pressed against the stone.

PATIENCE

There is a room now
    buried
in late morning
    sunlight
that will not
    change

in which a woman
    & a small
girl who is not
    me
although I am
    her patience

are ironing
    that life's
clothes & linens, themselves,
    even then,
inherited & handed
    down

and which now
    I can go
to my cupboard
    & smell
still, theirs a
    coolness

flesh can't have. There
    an open door
lets in a perfect shaft
    of light,
the rudder for
    the scene,

lets in the scent of
        the wisteria
trying once again
        to graft
onto the cypress tree
        out back,

and the smell of the pods
        of that tree
which look like the
        buttons
on the shirt we are
        ironing

my father is waiting for. . . .
        Someone
is raking the gravel.
        The cicadas
are just slowing
        down for

midmorning. We iron to find
        the parts
in each thing, making
        a tidy body
that folds away
        into itself,

& even our shadows, those other
        bodies
breaking & unbreaking
        against
the white walls, remain, blazing,
        in the draft

between the two open
    doors. Tell me
where that room is now,
    that stubborn
fragrant bloom? The fragile stem
    from here

to there is tragedy, I know,
    the path we
feed it by until it cracks
    open at last
& it's all right Maria is
    so tired

even the sweetness of
    wisteria
hurts, all right she has
    just lost
her son, a policeman, &
    is crying

as she irons, while I
    keep fingering
the ugly twistings of
    the wicker
hamper thinking was it
    really

living vine there once
    beneath,
& pain & hurrying
    & light
grow equal and become
    at last—

as if themselves beneath
    the blue
and eye-shaped
     iron—
the style,
    the innocence.

for John

MAKING A LIVING

Sometimes it is as easy as defining the common boundaries
of night and day. Because they are too easily apart;
even in the blurred hem of dusk and dawn
the white lake goes here,
the dark between
the pinecone lips

goes there. . . .
The hawks that fly only at night, for instance,
lay eggs directly on the hardest open ground,
a kind of night. And, looking for those eggs, imagine me
a kind of sunlight rising over
every hill. We think

that if what keeps us separate were found, it would dissolve.
It makes us feel our thinking is less cruel.
I see, we say, wishing the daylit distances
to be the terrain of the mind,
something you can own
by crossing,

not *I am seen*, or *can you see me?* Sometimes I'll take binoculars.
I love it when it all goes flat, and leaves and clouds
are instances of one idea—
for such is night, I think,
while day is how far
one must go

to connect parts. A man I loved
needed to pin me down when we made love.
Imagine us to be a kind of music box—that someone owned us,
opened us up; the pain
a knot we tied between our two good lengths
of privacy,

the way we agreed
to forego understanding. For love is to become, like pain,
at last opaque. And I believed that we, the parts, needed the whole,
its government, its appetite for us,
its love. As for the bird
that waits

at the boundary of these other, truer, lovers: *finding*
and *being found*—in their endless desire for one another,
I am what keeps them apart.

THE DAFFODIL

with its neck broken in two
    places has outlived
the others. It sees the floor,
    plays to the audience
of motes its head deflects.
    It's so still

it's a sundial. Across the room
    the three good ones
cluck in the sunlight.
    Their water darkens
though to us it looks
    clear. Around them

the room decides itself,
    rip-tide at my feet
called forever, now,
    a reason for stopping
where I do. You are
    elsewhere

who picked them with me,
    or, rather, watched me
rip them from the bed.
    When I broke this one,
sliding it through my palm
    like time till it snapped,

I wanted to say, I *am*
    careful, this is
great love, this catch
    as my thumb comes
too close. You looked away
    like the owl

who snapped against my windowpane.
    He dove into my darker
daylight for a world
    with a boundary

so you know when you've entered.
    Inside, we keep turning

up splinters. I think of you
    watching me, seeing
what's here slipping out of
    what it represents.
I think of what you
    have to overlook

to see me. Will the dust
    leave a flower
shaped like these yellow
    wings where it
has not fallen because they
    have not fallen?

FOR JOHN KEATS

Today, with a friend, in an archaic yellow light, I visited
   the graveyard
here, an easy lawn behind the school. This town knows where
to find its dead, it seems, the graves just flat stone markers
in the grass, a gap
where growth

is barely held back for a name. And it was difficult
   to know
where not to walk. To measure out and skip a length, a human
length, and just an extra bit, in case
or in respect
seemed right

and yet the plots, then, overlapped. Tell me where
   it's right
to walk? Here and there cut flowers had taken root
by accident. I recognized some Asphodels, Grandmother's
Pocketbooks. . . . How would you cross
a lawn that is

a sky? I skipped from name to name,
leaving a gap for limbs, for sleep, using my shadow as
a guage. But it was warm and windy, Spring, my skirts playing
my legs, and swallows
hugged the ground

in flight. What is respect? If we are gods up here,
sunny and quick in this Maylight, mindlight,
we are indecorous, we break every
enframement, being
entirely

transitive,
striding from rib to rib, or is it—since we're up here—
   thought
to thought? I played them all, therefore—limbs, names,
flowers, years, even the fresh plots
waiting to graft. We live up here

by blurring boundaries, calling it *love, the present moment,* or
the beautiful. We live a harsh fecundity, it seems
to me, the symbol tripping much
        too freely
over everything
it signifies.

(*with Nanette*)

WOOD WASPS IN THE
SPANISH WILLOW

Although it doesn't seem
    anything's missing,
thousands of wasps
    have eaten
intelligently
    of these branches

and made, out of spittle
    and pulp
a fine grey paper
    they've bandaged
sheet after sheet
    round and under and through

the branchings
    until it's
a nest, a dark grey
    freedom.
What they do
    is the work

of reason, making
    of the willow-wood, the given,
by interrupting it
    and letting it cross
the numinous
    body,

another wood,
    finer, more
volatile,
    something that traps
and seals
    an emptiness,

the meaning of the willow tree,
    its animal. . . .

2.

In Goya, too, fate
    floats, just above
the landscape
    of our lives,
the same color
    as our lives,

the same dark color—three crones,
    a cloud,
spun out of what evolves
    beneath them,
the silver river
    dividing the land

where here and there light
    touches
something dark into something
    glistening
for no reason.
    How helpless they are,

spinning and cutting.
    They need
the solitude
    that wades out beneath them
into the river
    hoping for fish.

One of them holds
    the delicate scissors
up into
    the sky. How free
it is, below them, the tree,
    the plotline,

branching this way
    and that

in the warm summer wind.
     He casts out
a bit further.
     Let them spin

something perfect
     and useful
out of his waiting.

3.

El Destino, he'll call it, madman,
     on his hands and knees
in the Quinta del Sordo
     rubbing the paint, the black-greens,
the deep
     greens

into the walls, spelling out
     into the paint
"the dream of reason
     produces
monsters." On
     the other side

of his wall
     in a hot sun
the morning glory vine
     presses easily
back.
     How far apart

things seem
     to it
who would seize them
     into its body
making a world that's whole
     though wholly buried

under its scaled
       green flesh.
By summer's end
       it will be
seamless. Are they
       more true,

the cracks, the shutters, the rotting
       fenceposts
it has connected
       for the design
that governs them,
       or saved

in the loss
       of uselessness?

EROSION

I would not want, I think, a higher intelligence, one
simultaneous, cut clean
of sequence. No,
it is our slowness I love, growing slower,
tapping the paintbrush against the visible,
tapping the mind.
We are, ourselves, a mannerism now,
having fallen
out of the chain
of evolution.
So we grow fat with unqualified life.
Today, on this beach
I am history to these fine
pebbles. I run them
through my fingers. Each time
some molecules rub off
evolving into
the invisible. Always
I am trying to feel
the erosion—my grandfather, stiffening
on his bed, learning
to float on time, his mind like bait presented
to the stream ongoing, or you, by my side,
sleep rinsing you always a little less
clean, or daily
the erosion
of the right word, what it shuts,
or the plants coming forth as planned out my window, row
after row, sealed
into here. . . .
I've lined all our wineglasses up on the sill,
a keyboard, a garden. Flowers of the poles.
I'm gifting each with a little less water.
You can tap them

for music.
Outside the window it's starting to snow.
It's going to get colder.
The less full the glass, the truer
the sound.
This is my song
for the North
coming toward us.

LOVE

Here it's harvest. Dust
    coarsens
the light. In the heat
    in the distance
the men burn
    their fields

to heal them. The grass
    is tall.
They disappear,
    they reappear . . .
slowly they navigate
    by fire,

cutting a path
    of ash.
They beat
    the flames
then lean
    on their tall forks

and stare. Nearby
    the sheep
in a stunned unison
    work what
remains. Dogs bite
    the strays.

What stark thing
    is it
we want
    that's only visible, believable,
caught through
    this blinding

yield? What poverty
        is strict enough?
Eight hundred years
        ago
in these fields
        the man

known as Saint
        Francis
abandoned by his
        church
and going blind
        spent all

one night. The medicine,
        the light
of his time,
        saw fit to burn him
at the temples
        to restore sight,

and all the tiny veins
        from ear to eye,
out of tremendous love,
        were cut.
It didn't work,
        but in great pain

near here, one night,
        the story goes,
rats worried him,
        visiting
his helpless warmth.
        To see them

for what they were,
     old man,
he composed
     in the dark
his famous
     canticle—*brother*

sunlight, brother
     firelight. The rats
traveled his face
     eating
the open scars. Later
     his blessèd

aides bore through both ears
     with red hot irons
to no avail
     for sight. *Harm not*
the fire
     he said

to those who would
     save him,
and never would he, did he,
     extinguish
a candle,
     a lantern,

with so much
     pity
was he moved
     toward it.

TWO PAINTINGS
BY GUSTAV KLIMT

Although what glitters
    on the trees
row after perfect row,
    is merely
the injustice
    of the world,

the chips on the bark of each
    beech tree
catching the light, the sum
    of these delays
is the beautiful, the human
    beautiful,

body of flaws.
    The dead
would give anything
    I'm sure,
to step again onto
    the leafrot,

into the avenue of mottled shadows,
    the speckled
broken skins. The dead
    in their sheer
open parenthesis, what they
    wouldn't give

for something to lean on
    that won't
give way. I think I
    would weep
for the moral nature
    of this world,

for right and wrong like pools
    of shadow
and light you can step in
    and out of
crossing this yellow beech forest,
    this *buchen-wald*,

one autumn afternoon, late
    in the twentieth
century, in hollow light,
    in gaseous light. . . .
To receive the light
    and return it

and stand in rows, anonymous,
    is a sweet secret
even the air wishes
    it could unlock.
See how it pokes at them
    in little hooks,

the blue air, the yellow trees.
    Why be afraid?
They say when Klimt
    died suddenly
a painting, still
    incomplete,

was found in his studio,
    a woman's body
open at its point of
    entry,
rendered in graphic,
    pornographic,

detail—something like
    a scream
between her legs. Slowly,
    feathery,
he had begun to paint
    a delicate

garment (his trademark)
    over this mouth
of her body. The mouth
    of her face
is genteel, bored, feigning a need
    for sleep. The fabric

defines the surface,
    the story,
so we are drawn to it,
    its blues
and yellows glittering
    like a stand

of beech trees late
    one afternoon
in Germany, in fall.
    It is called
Buchenwald, it is
    1890. In

the finished painting
    the argument
has something to do
    with pleasure.

HISTORY

Into whose ear the deeds are spoken. The only
listener. So I believed
he would remember everything, the murmuring trees,
the sunshine's zealotry, its deep
unevenness. For history
is the opposite
of the eye
for whom, for instance, six million bodies in portions
of hundreds and
the flowerpots broken by a sudden wind stand as
equivalent. What more
is there
than fact? *I'll give ten thousand dollars to the man*
who proves the holocaust really
occurred said the exhausted solitude
in San Francisco
in 1980. Far in the woods
in a faded photograph
in 1942 the man with his own
genitalia in his mouth and hundreds of
slow holes
a pitchfork has opened
over his face
grows beautiful. The ferns and deepwood
lilies catch
the eye. Three men in ragged uniforms
with guns keep laughing
nervously. They share the day
with him. A bluebird
sings. The feathers of the shade touch every inch
of skin—the hand holding down the delicate gun,
the hands holding down the delicate
hips. And the sky
is visible between the men, between
the trees, a blue spirit
cnveloping
anything. Late in the story, in Northern Italy,

a man cuts down some trees for winter
fuel. We read this in the evening
news. Watching the fire burn late
one night, watching it change and change, a hand
   grenade,
lodged in the pulp the young tree
grew around, explodes, blinding the man, killing
his wife. Now who
will tell the children
fairytales? The ones where simple
crumbs over the forest
floor endure
to help us home?

MASACCIO'S EXPULSION

Is this really the failure
    of silence,
or eternity, where these two
    suffer entrance
into the picture
    plane,

a man and woman
    so hollowed
by grief they cover
    their eyes
in order not to see
    the inexhaustible grammar

before them—labor, judgement,
    saints and peddlers—
the daylight hopelessly even
    upon them,
and our eyes. But this too
    is a garden

I'd say, with its architecture
    of grief,
its dark and light
    in the folds
of clothing, and oranges
    for sale

among the shadows
    of oranges. All round them,
on the way down
    toward us,
woods thicken. And perhaps
    it is a flaw

on the wall of this church, or age,
    or merely the restlessness
of the brilliant
    young painter,

the large blue bird
        seen flying too low

just where the trees
        clot. I
want to say to them
        who have crossed
into this terrifying
        usefulness—symbols,

balancing shapes in
        a composition,
mother and father,
        hired hands—
I want to say to them,
        Take your faces

out of your hands,
        look at that bird,
the gift of
        the paint—
I've seen it often
        here

in my life,
        a Sharp-Shinned Hawk,
tearing into the woods
        for which it's
too big, abandoning
        the open

prairie in which
        it is free and easily
eloquent. Watch
        where it will not
veer but follows
        the stain

of woods,
        a long blue arc
breaking itself
        through the wet
black ribs
        of those trees,

seeking a narrower
        place. Always
I find the feathers
        afterward. . . .
Perhaps you know
        why it turns in

this way
        and will not stop?
In the foreground
        almost life-size
the saints hawk their wares,
        and the women,

and merchants. They too
        are traveling
a space too small
        to fit in,
calling out names
        or prices

or proof of faith.
        Whatever they are,
it beats
        up through the woods
of their bodies,
        almost a light, up

through their fingertips,
    their eyes.
There isn't a price
    (that floats up
through their miraculous
    bodies

and lingers above them
    in the gold air)
that won't live forever.

UPDRAFT

(New York City, May 1982)

1.

You who are not different,
let the hush and click of the heady leaves, the avenues
    announcing rain
and the hum of the neon
and the miraculous ropings of spittle and dead
    leaves and urine
and new rain
               in the gutters

stick to You. Let them in. They are Your cellwork,
    dividing,
inventing. And the old woman in my basement rooms
    with her whine
and her knife.
And all the blossoms ripped suddenly by one gust, one
updraft—mosaic

of dust and silks
by which we are all rising, turning, all
free

2.

crossing against the light.
As if the veil, the earth-dress, hem, were turning, sleeve
    of the vast
lifting. . . . Is she

bored? Is she sleepy? All the statistics, the century's
    burned and gang-raped
turning, lifting, a blade catching the late
light

redeeming it, and us needing its wrongest beauty, coherent
    refusals. . . . Does that
acquit us, that starched, intelligent
    love,

does that make her a good

girl when the lights come on, deep and bloody in the late
      news,
and the day, the luminous silk, seems to leak out
      through the purr
of the flesh, unquenched, girl, in her

puddles and black silks
with red and electric
blues, will she

be good
and worth us, for sale as she is, even the last spit and wrapper
saying Sorry in dawns that gleam and suck
the life out of you,

                    3.

so that we need to lean and rub against what isn't thought.
How clean the leaves become then. How clean
the heart is finally, becoming what
it cannot change.

As the blood smears itself against the mind.
And cannot go further.
Our chilly mother-gap. Held breath. Unpromised land.
Meanwhile listen to the flies, the crones,

everywhere threading and threading, contagion, hope. . . .
For in their mouths
the whole world passes, is
repaired, against the light, so let her slip

out of her heavy garment then, let her slip back
into the rib, into Your dream, Your
loneliness, back, deep into the undress, back
before Your needle leapt in Your fingers, meaning.

OF UNEVENNESS

this is our god, the Summer
    Solstice, yearly
buried, resurrected, the longest
    day. And what am I
to do with it, this fingerswidth
    of extra light

I am about to lose? What plant in it
    would grow? I'm on
my porch and staring into it. The jay
    that lives here
threads an extra fly or two tonight,
    no doubt. . . . The real

is a nation of such inroads—the jay
    on Indigo, the note he calls
on what I hear, inroads
    of being found
on being lost. Tomorrow
    this gift

will have gone under once again,
    and for a year
these hundred twenty seconds be
    the hinge, the buried
quick, what throws the rest of each day
    off enough

to make it run. The quick given the jay
    is glut
of blue, and to the rose the extra
    given is the bloom,
the wading out into delay. And to
    the mind

this almost wholly lifting hem
    is given.
And though I can't see any more
    today
than yesterday, it's true, I can
    push out

and take root in that tiny space
    which is as far,
precisely, as the visible will ever go,
    while the progressive
loss of light from here on in
    is runner, stem,

and, in the darkest instance, blossom to
    this narrow tract,
this buried, infinite precision,
    this heaven. . . .

AT LUCA SIGNORELLI'S
RESURRECTION OF THE BODY

See how they hurry
    to enter
their bodies,
    these spirits.
Is it better, flesh,
    that they

should hurry so?
    From above
the green-winged angels
    blare down
trumpets and light. But
    they don't care,

they hurry to congregate,
    they hurry
into speech, until
    it's a marketplace,
it is humanity. But still
    we wonder

in the chancel
    of the dark cathedral,
is it better, back?
    The artist
has tried to make it so: each tendon
    they press

to re-enter
    is perfect. But is it
perfection
    they're after,
pulling themselves up
    through the soil

into the weightedness, the color,
    into the eye

of the painter? Outside
        it is 1500,
all round the cathedral
        streets hurry to open

through the wild
        silver grasses. . . .
The men and women
        on the cathedral wall
do not know how,
        having come this far,

to stop their
        hurrying. They amble off
in groups, in
        couples. Soon
some are clothed, there is
        distance, there is

perspective. Standing below them
        in the church
in Orvieto, how can we
        tell them
to be stern and brazen
        and slow,

that there is no
        entrance,
only entering. They keep on
        arriving,
wanting names,
        wanting

happiness. In his studio
        Luca Signorelli
in the name of God
        and Science
and the believable
        broke into the body

studying arrival.
    But the wall
of the flesh
    opens endlessly,
its vanishing point so deep
    and receding

we have yet to find it,
    to have it
stop us. So he cut
    deeper,
graduating slowly
    from the symbolic

to the beautiful. How far
    is true?
When his one son
    died violently,
he had the body brought to him
    and laid it

on the drawing-table,
    and stood
at a certain distance
    awaiting the best
possible light, the best depth
    of day,

then with beauty and care
    and technique
and judgement, cut into
    shadow, cut
into bone and sinew and every
    pocket

in which the cold light
    pooled.
It took him days
    that deep
caress, cutting,
     unfastening,

until his mind
    could climb into
the open flesh and
    mend itself.

THE SENSE OF AN ENDING

There in the sound of the chainsaw winding down. The crack
of the young trees a distant

neighbor needs to clear. A slamming
door. The freeway whining when the wind

turns down this way. There in the undulant cawing way above
of four ravens crossing back over

now that it's dusk (Somewhere for them is *in*
or *out*. Therefore they point that way.) And in the wind

making a sound that lifts the lilacs, releasing
scent, making a sound then

when it puts them back, a sound I cannot
hear,

the start of another scale,
sound or silence, the sound of the purple, tearing,

the sound of the wires we wrapped
to hold the branches right, sound

of my looking now. And then remembering.

*

Wherefore paradise is a walled garden signifying
delight. The wall of the flesh

that must be broken, now, always, over the miles by knee
on backroads to the holy

Guadeloupe. Signifying *delight*, so that it's best to load
the body's weight with gifts—breads, or sugared

bones, or better yet pregnant and far gone—so that the knees
   break open
further, taking in pebbles, the hair of nighttime animals whose skins

are almost dust, the dust of seeds, the dust of tiny rodent
bones, and nighthawk wings, and the claydust of the relics

these cornfields endlessly turn up—tearjars,
grainbreaks and everywhere the coins, the small portable

gods. Because the body must open
for its world

so that we know there is a wall
beyond which we can't go. So that, on the erosion-

line, bodies and antibodies, dust and
blood, we are defined by what we will not take

into ourselves. . . . Two cherubim
each with a flaming sword

placed evermore to guard the gates. One with his mouth
ajar. One sealed. . . .

*

You told me the wolf was wild and therefore even in
this cage larger than any natural

den would lose its mind. It's in
his turn. He'll pace allright but then look carefully

at how, reaching the edge, he turns around. It's
too precise. Too much clicks shut in that quick step

revolving on the one hind leg, bringing the other down just as
the swivel ends, then giving over all the weight

to one front paw, onto each pad distinctly it would

seem, then onto number four and he's
around headed the other way

again. It's beautiful. You can hear
minutes stitching shut. He's got it down to

breaths. A form. Finished each time by how
it starts again. And yet I thought it was freedom

this tightening of something wholly wild into
a wholly true

design. A narrowing. Until you see
the whole unseeable distance he must cross in just

one step. A narrowing,
our hero going back and forth and back and forth, or is it

forth and forth. . . . Will it be so?

*

As if there were a whole continent floating at all
times beneath us.

Over which we travel making
decisions.

Meanwhile, beneath, it is the flesh, the
unrecorded history: backyards, beginnings, faces, everything

with or without luck, weather, a fence
here and there coming down, going

up. Meanwhile, above, the dates are remembered. An act
here or there like ice over the long water is said

to change the course
of the story. . . . One night someone no longer comes home. One night

in a strong sooty wind a species of harbor grass
as yet unnamed goes extinct. A tiny category (poison

or remedy?). . . . As if that continent, though, in another's
book were the center of all

the action. As in the dark those small creatures
who are blind by day awaken because this is their

opening, this dark blue real in which a sound is
a motive, in which a scent

is the edge of a flesh, or itself a flesh,

in which something is chosen yet nothing excluded.

*

From childhood I still own the mornings at the poly—
clinic, the avenue of palms always in their warm

clattery wind. And the simple task, tuesdays and thursdays
with the eyemachines: two of each earthly thing, one to

each eye (rabbit or trumpet, apple
or rock) and the mind

given the task: to bring them
together. The heavy windows always open because

the city needs to capture
what air it can, what air won't move, and trap it

in buildings, and, window to window, turn it
to draft. Always in our houses

that good injustice, dusty, cooler, that imaginary wind
created wholly by wrongs, by

gaps. So the words of the palm came in. So the hiss of
noon over the umbrella pines and the long insuck

just as the cicadas started up again. So the
outside travels through the strange

indoors, back and forth, to correct
what we will not

correct. Joined by one lust, therefore—the two of us—housed
and unhoused—out of one long chord

of justice. Like a stain
traveling through us. This sleepy rocking back and forth and back

and forth for evenness; for evenness or parity,
a bridge over the river, or, better yet, no river

at all.

*

Or where the draft is from an unseen
gap. And translates through us, through

our flesh, our opening, a swift
and bloody

current. Because I think the human
souls are in a frenzy

to be born, to be brought over into here through flesh
through bone down into

time. Sometimes, on a day like today for instance, when
the heat is dry and gold and clicks

its dusty trees open and shut, when the cicadas
have done for the day and the distance whimpers

in gulls and dockpilings, some *times*
I can feel them pressing into my human frame, knocking,

pushing, as if an entrance into here, no matter
how short or broken—no matter

the hundred kinds of burn, the thousand kinds
of rot—no matter

the terrible insufficiencies of matter in the face
of any kind of spent

time, were better than any
freedom, any wholeness—horribly better—even for a

single hour, no matter what,
even for minutes, better, this heaviness, this stilled

quickness, this skin, this line
all the way round and sealed into the jagged island

form, the delicate
ending, better, even for an instant, even if never brought

further than term
into this broken mewing, this dust of lilacs, cawing

ravens, door just slamming, someone
suddenly home in this lie we call blue light.

PRINCETON SERIES
OF CONTEMPORARY POETS